NAME YOUR EMOTIONS

SOMETIMES I FEEL ANXIOUS

by Jaclyn Jaycox

PEBBLE
a capstone imprint

Pebble Emerge is published by Pebble, an imprint of Capstone.
1710 Roe Crest Drive
North Mankato, Minnesota 56003
www.capstonepub.com

Library of Congress Cataloging-in-Publication Data is available on the
Library of Congress website.
ISBN 978-1-9771-2469-2 (library binding)
ISBN 978-1-9771-2645-0 (paperback)
ISBN 978-1-9771-2512-5 (eBook PDF)

Summary: What does it mean to be anxious? It's an emotion everyone
has. Children will learn how to recognize when they are feeling anxious
and examples of good ways to manage their emotion. A mindfulness
activity will give kids the opportunity to practice managing their
feelings.

Image Credits
Getty Images: Flying Colours Ltd, 15; Shutterstock: Ann in the uk, 19,
Asier Romero, Cover, Bobex-73, 6, Color Symphony, Design Element,
Daniel Jedzura, 9, Ewa Leon, 21, fizkes, 12, Jan H Andersen, 5, MC42,
17, Monkey Business Images, 13, Rob Marmion, 11, Samuel Borges
Photography, 18, Sketchphoto, 7

Editorial Credits
Designer: Kay Fraser; Media Researcher: Tracy Cummins; Production
Specialist: Katy LaVigne

Printed and bound in China.
3322

TABLE OF CONTENTS

Words in **bold** are in the glossary.

WHAT IS ANXIETY?

Your friend invites you over for your first sleepover. You are excited! But then you start to worry. Does your friend have a night-light like yours? What if you get scared and your parents aren't there? You might be anxious. Anxiety is an **emotion**.

5

WHAT DOES IT FEEL LIKE TO BE ANXIOUS?

Try to think of a time you were anxious. Was it your first day of school? Maybe it was before your first soccer game. How did you feel?

When you are anxious, your heart beats fast. You get shaky. Your hands can get sweaty. You get butterflies in your stomach. You may have trouble eating or sleeping.

USING YOUR SENSES

Everyone has five **senses**. People can touch, taste, see, hear, and smell things. Your senses send messages to your brain. That's where feelings start.

Seeing a storm coming might make you anxious. Hearing a fire alarm go off can make you feel this way too.

9

TALKING ABOUT YOUR FEELINGS

It's important to talk about your feelings. If you are anxious, tell someone you care about. Talk to them about why you feel this way. They can find ways to help you feel better. Talking about it can help you calm down too.

UNDERSTANDING ANXIETY

Anxiety is a feeling of fear. It is caused by something **stressful** or scary. This feeling is kind of like a wave. It can build up and feel really big. But then it slowly starts to fade.

You might feel like this before giving a report in front of the class. You may worry about making a mistake. But you feel much calmer when you are done.

Anxiety can make you feel bad. But it can be a useful emotion. This feeling can keep you safe. You might feel anxious around people you don't know. It helps you remember the dangers of talking to strangers.

HANDLING YOUR FEELINGS

Anxiety can be a strong feeling. It's important to know how to handle it. You don't want this feeling to last too long. It can **affect** your daily life. It makes it hard to think about other things. You may not want to do things that give you this feeling.

17

You can take deep breaths to **relax**. Think about happy things. You can take a walk outside. Read your favorite book. Play a game.

You can draw or write down things that make you anxious. Read them out loud. Then tear them up and throw them away.

MINDFULNESS ACTIVITY

Sometimes anxious feelings can make it hard to relax. Grab a pinwheel and try this fun activity to calm your body and mind.

What You Do:

1. Hold a pinwheel near your mouth.

2. Take a slow, deep breath and hold it in for two seconds.

3. Slowly let the breath out, blowing on the pinwheel.

4. Repeat until you feel calm and relaxed.

GLOSSARY

affect (uh-FEKT)—to influence or change someone or something

emotion (i-MOH-shuhn)—a strong feeling; people have and show emotions such as happiness, sadness, fear, anger, and jealousy

relax (ri-LAKS)—to calm down

sense (SENSS)—a way of knowing about your surroundings; hearing, smelling, touching, tasting, and sight are the five senses

stress (STRES)—mental or emotional pressure

READ MORE

Kreul, Holde. *My Feelings and Me*. New York: Skyhorse Publishing, 2018.

Willey, Kira. *Mindfulness Moments for Kids: Breathe Like a Bear*. New York: Penguin Random House, 2019.

INTERNET SITES

Kids' Health – Relax & Unwind Center
kidshealth.org/EN/Kids/stress-center?WT.ac=k-ra

Kids' Health – Talking About Your Feelings
kidshealth.org/en/kids/talk-feelings.html?WT.ac=ctg

INDEX